MAKERS OF INDIA

MAKERS OF INDIA

ASOKA MAURYA
SRI HARSHA OF KANAUJ
AKBAR, THE GREAT MOGUL
SIVAJI THE MARATHA
MAHARAJA RANJIT SINGH
SIR SAIYID AHMED KHAN
MAHATMA GANDHI

by
HUGH GEORGE RAWLINSON

Essay Index Reprint Series

  BOOKS FOR LIBRARIES PRESS
FREEPORT, NEW YORK

First published as part of the Living Names Series

Copyright 1942

Reprinted 1971 by arrangement with
Oxford University Press

DS434
R35

INTERNATIONAL STANDARD BOOK NUMBER:
0-8369-2251-4

LIBRARY OF CONGRESS CATALOG CARD NUMBER:
77-134126

PRINTED IN THE UNITED STATES OF AMERICA

ASOKA MAURYA

IN the fifth century before Christ, there arose in Eastern India the mighty empire of Magadha, with its capital at Pataliputra, not far from the modern city of Patna. In 325 B.C., a young man named Chandragupta was banished by the reigning king. He fled to the Punjab, where he met the great Greek Emperor Alexander. After Alexander's departure, he returned and stirred up a rebellion among the people of Magadha, and, with the aid of a minister named Chanakya, he overthrew the monarch and had himself made king. He was very fond of the Greeks, and married a Greek princess. There was always a Greek ambassador in the Court, and in this way India became acquainted with the civilization of the West.

Chandragupta made Pataliputra into a splendid city. It was surrounded by a deep moat, which drained into the river Son. Behind the moat was a wall of wooden logs, for stone was very little used in those days. There were drawbridges, gates and towers at regular intervals. Inside the walls the city was well laid out, with wide, straight roads, temples and market places. The bazaars were filled with silks, muslins, brocades, steel weapons, drugs and perfumes, ivory work, jewellery, and gold and silver ornaments. They were thronged with merchants and travellers from all parts of the world. A special board of officers, like the municipality of these days, controlled the trade and the affairs of the city. It fixed rates of wages, stamped the weights and measures, and regulated prices. Any merchant who tried to sell old goods as new was severely punished. Another board saw that the streets were kept clean, and arranged for putting out fires. The people were prosperous and contented. There were theatres and racecourses, and there were plenty of amusements in the shape of plays, dancing, horse and chariot racing, and fights between wild animals. On festivals, the streets were illuminated very much as they are at Divali to-day. The citizens loved gaily coloured clothes, and they lived chiefly on rice. Women were well treated, and though the right of *Suttee* was practised, it was voluntary. Greek travellers said that the Hindus were noted for their truthfulness and honesty. No Indian was ever convicted of lying, and it was not necessary to have witnesses for legal documents. Houses were left unguarded, and in the whole of Chandragupta's army, there were no convictions for thefts of over 100 rupees.

In the centre of the city was the Royal Palace. It stood in the midst of a spacious park, full of rare trees, with peacocks, deer, and other birds and animals. There were many lakes, stocked with sacred fish. The palace was built of wood, and the pillars were overlaid with plates of gold and silver, beautifully engraved. The King worked very hard; he rose at dawn, and after saying his prayers he saw his ministers, and then went to the hall of audience where he heard complaints. He was a very strict ruler, and many attempts were made to murder him. In order to avoid this, he never slept twice in the same bed, and he was constantly surrounded by a guard of Amazons or female warriors, who had orders to cut down anyone who approached too close.

On the occasion of religious festivals, the king, surrounded by his guards, went in procession through the city. He was followed by hosts of attendants in holiday clothes, carrying gold and copper vessels set with precious stones. Others bore rich robes, or led tame beasts, such as leopards, lions, buffaloes and elephants, or carried rare birds in gilded cages. After a long and prosperous reign, Chandragupta retired from the world and became a Jain monk, leaving the crown to his son Bindusara, who also was a great conqueror.

Asoka, who succeeded to the throne in 273 B.C., ruled at first very much in the same way as his father and grandfather. He had a vast army, consisting of elephants, chariots, cavalry and infantry, 600,000 men in all. The Indian bowmen were particularly skilful, and they could pierce an iron shield with their arrows. In 261 B.C. Asoka set out to conquer the last remaining independent kingdom in northern India. This was Kalinga or

Orissa, a wild, wooded country on the east coast, between the Godaveri and Mahanadi rivers. The Orissans loved their independence, and fought fiercely for it. Asoka's troops behaved with great cruelty; 125,000 people were taken prisoners, 100,000 were slain, and many times that number were rendered homeless. No mercy was shown, and neither Brahmins, women, old people nor little children were spared.

Just at that time, Asoka made the acquaintance of a Buddhist teacher, named Upagupta. Upagupta instructed him in the teaching of the Lord Buddha; and especially he pointed out to him the doctrine of *Ahimsa* or harmlessness; it was above all things wrong to take life, whether of men or of animals. Asoka was at once filled with remorse at the thought of what his armies had done in Orissa, and he vowed that he would never go to war again. In future, the war-drum would sound no more in the land. The only drum would be that which proclaimed the Dhamma or Law of Piety. 'If a hundredth, nay a thousandth part of the persons who were then slain, carried away captive, or done to death, were now to suffer the same fate, it would be a matter of remorse to His Majesty,' he declared.

As time went on, Asoka became more and more strict. He actually took the yellow robes of a Buddhist monk, though he still remained Emperor. He was determined that all his people should hear the teaching of the Buddha. 'Everywhere in my dominions, the Commissioners and District Officers every five years must proceed on circuit, not only to execute their ordinary duties, but to give instruction in the Law.' In order that the people might understand, edicts were engraved in places where they would be most likely to attract the attention of passers-by.

The Law, as taught by the Emperor to his people, was quite simple to understand. True religion, he said, consisted in observing four great rules: honouring one's father and mother; liberality to friends, relations, holy men and Brahmins; abstention from the slaughter of any living creature; and kindness to slaves and servants. 'What is the Law of Piety?' he asks. 'It lies in good deeds, compassion, liberality, truthfulness and purity.' Above all things, men must observe strict religious toleration. 'A man must not revere his own religion and condemn that of his neighbour. Other people's beliefs deserve respect for one reason or another.'

The Emperor practised what he preached. His life was that of the ordinary monk or *Bhikku*; he gave up the splendours and luxuries of the Court, as the Lord Buddha had done before him, and contented himself with a single yellow robe, a needle to mend it, a razor to shave his head, a strainer lest he should destroy life in his drinking water, and a begging bowl. In the eleventh year of his reign, he stopped the royal hunts, and forbade animal sacrifices. Asoka never spared himself.

'I must work for the public benefit,' he said. 'For what do I toil? For the discharge of my debt to all living beings, so that I may make them happy in this world, and sure of heaven in the next.' Trees were planted and wells dug at roadsides, resthouses and hospitals were erected for man and beast. The Buddhist monasteries provided a liberal education for rich and poor. Especial measures were taken for the protection of the poor jungle tribes, who were often treated by high caste Hindus as outcasts. Another merciful act on the part of the great Emperor was in the treatment of prisoners. Criminals were released on various occasions, and those under sentence of death were given a respite of several days, during which holy men visited them and prepared their souls for the next world.

Asoka was not content merely to preach his religion in his own country. He was anxious to spread it all over the world. Buddhist missionaries went, not only to every part of India, but to his Greek friends in the distant West. To Ceylon especially, he sent his son and daughter, Mahinda and Sanghamitta, with a branch of the sacred Bodhi tree under which the Lord Buddha was sitting when He attained Buddhahood. The Buddhist missionaries received a warm welcome from the Sinhalese King Tissa, and he and all his Court were converted. The branch of the Bodhi tree was planted at Anuradhapura, the capital, where it still grows. Buddhism, long dead in the land of India, still flourishes in the beautiful island of Ceylon. The missionaries brought with them the culture of their own land, especially the arts of stone-carving and irrigation, and in a lovely hillside are still shown Mahinda's cell and tomb.

In 249 B.C., the twenty-third year of his reign, Asoka, accompanied by his teacher Upagupta, made a pilgrimage to the Holy Places. He visited the Lumbini Garden, where the Blessed One was born, and Kapilavastu where He spent His boyhood. From there he visited the Deer Garden at Benares where He preached His first sermon, and 'set the wheel of the Law rolling', Sravasti where He spent so many years, Gaya where under the tree He received His call, and, lastly, Kusinagara where He attained Nirvana and was cremated. At all these places Asoka erected lofty stone pillars with lion capitals, and colleges for the study and teaching of the Law of Piety. On his return, he called a Council which drew up a correct list of the Buddhist Scriptures.

Asoka was a great builder. Formerly only wood was employed by Indian architects; Asoka introduced the use of stone, and his workmen learnt to carve and polish stone pillars in a most exquisite manner. All over the country were Buddhist monasteries, and the yellow-robed monks worked among the people, educating them and preaching to them, and nursing them when they were sick. In order to accommodate them during the rainy season, spacious cave-dwellings, known as Vihâras, were excavated out of the hillsides. The walls were often decorated with paintings representing scenes in the life of the Buddha. Stupas or mounds were constructed to hold relics of the Master; these were surrounded by stone railings with gateways exquisitely carved. Shortly before his death, Asoka retired from the world and left his kingdom to his two grandsons. He passed away in 232 B.C. His reign is the brightest spot in the history of the world, and there is no doubt that he was many centuries in advance of his time. To-day, when the world is full of bloodshed and violence, it is sad to think that twenty-one centuries ago there was actually a great ruler who tried to govern his vast Empire, stretching from one end of India to the other, without an army and without the use of force. Asoka was in this respect the greatest king that the world has known.

SRI HARSHA OF KANAUJ

HARSHA VARDHANA

At the end of the sixth century after Christ, Northern India was in a very disturbed state. It was broken up into a number of small kingdoms, and the country was being ravaged by the Huns, fierce Mongolian horsemen from Central Asia. At that time a Raja named Prabhakara Vardhana was ruling at the holy city of Thanesar, not far from where Delhi now stands. He had two sons, Rajya Vardhana and Harsha, and a daughter named Rajyasri. The boys were educated as all princes were at that time. They learned to ride and wield the sword and shoot with the bow. The girl was taught singing, dancing and other feminine arts, and in due time was wedded to Prince Grahavarman, son of the ruler of a neighbouring state.

One day news arrived that the Huns were once more ravaging the land. The king was growing old, but he told his elder son Rajya to put on his armour and drive out the intruders. Harsha was too young to take the field, but followed at a distance with the cavalry. He spent his time in shooting lions, tigers and boars in the neighbouring jungles. While he was thus engaged, a messenger rode up at full speed, and, jumping from his sweating horse, announced that the old king was dangerously ill with fever. Harsha at once set out for the capital, and for three days did not even stop to take food. He arrived just before his father died, and at once sent couriers on swift camels to summon his brother. Rajya Vardhana at last returned, his arms still wrapped in the long white bandages which covered the arrow-wounds he had received in combat with the Huns. The two brothers were devoted friends, and each wanted the other to succeed. But of course the elder son had to ascend the throne, and was proclaimed Raja.

Just at that moment, fresh bad tidings arrived. The wicked king of Malwa had invaded the territory of their brother-in-law, Prince Grahavarman, and slain him, and had carried off their sister in fetters. Rajya Vardhana set out at full speed to punish the murderer, leaving Harsha behind to manage the kingdom. Harsha chafed greatly at this, and could scarcely make the time pass: he was like 'a wild elephant which had strayed from the herd'. One day, as he sat in the audience chamber, a cavalry officer entered, covered with dust and greatly dejected. He announced that Rajya Vardhana had routed his foes with ease, but afterwards, having been lured to a conference by the king of the Gaudas, weaponless, confiding and alone, he was treacherously put to death. Harsha now had a double task, to avenge his brother's death and to rescue his sister. He assembled a great army, and swore an oath ' by the dust of his father's feet ', that unless in a few days he cleared the earth of the Gaudas, and made it resound with the clank of the fetters on their ankles, he would hurl himself on a funeral pyre ' as a moth does on an oil-fed flame '.

As the young king was riding with his cavalry through the Malwa forest, he met a party of beggars who told him that on that very morning they had seen a beautiful princess going to her funeral pyre, accompanied by her maidens. They begged him to go and prevent her from carrying out her purpose. Harsha galloped at full speed to the spot. As he approached an open glade, he heard some faint but piteous cries, and found that it was none other than Rajyasri, on the very point of entering the flames. He snatched her away and carried her to the foot of a tree; presently some water was brought, and she recovered. Brother and sister were overjoyed at meeting once more, and they returned to the capital, leaving the commander-in-chief, Bhandi, to carry out the task of punishing the wicked Gaudas.

Harsha, however, was not content to stay idle for very long. He was determined to make himself Emperor of the whole of India. For the next six years he went from east to west, subduing all who refused to obey him. During all these years, the elephants were not unharnessed and the soldiers did not take off their armour. But there was one part of the country which he was unable to enter. This was the Maharashtra or country of the Marathas, ruled over at that time by a king, known as Pulakesi, of the Chalukya clan. The Marathas were even then famous for their valour. We are told they had hundreds of war elephants, which in time of battle were made drunk with wine. Then, rushing forward in a mass, the elephants would trample down all before them, and no enemy could stand up to them. Another custom of the Marathas was, when a general lost a war, to present him with women's clothes. The general was so ashamed that he was driven to seek death for himself in battle. Be this as it may, Harsha could not advance over the Vindhya mountains, as they are covered with dense jungle, where his chariots were of little use. On his return, Harsha determined to build himself a new capital at Kanauj on the Ganges. He made here a very handsome city, four miles long and a mile broad. It had lofty buildings, tanks full of lotuses and sacred fish, and parks and gardens for the citizens. There were over one hundred Buddhist monasteries and many Hindu temples.

It was a very common thing at this time for pilgrims from China to come to India, in order to visit the places sacred to the memory of the Lord Buddha. The most celebrated of these was a learned Chinaman of the name of Huien Tsang, or Yuan Chuang, 'the Master of the Law'. He came all the way from China across the Gobi desert, and then over the mountain passes into North-West

India. On his journey, he nearly lost his life many times; he almost died of thirst, his caravan was attacked by brigands, and he had to cross the Himalaya mountains by passes many thousands of feet high, often blocked by snow and ice and rushing torrents. He reached India in A.D. 630 and stayed for fifteen years.

Huien Tsang wrote a very interesting account of Harsha's Empire. He says that it was divided into a number of provinces, each with its governor and officials. But the king saw personally all that was going on. He was a tireless worker, and the day was too short for him. Except in the rainy season, he toured from one end of his kingdom to the other, never staying long in one place. While on tour, he lived very simply in huts made of grass and bamboo, which were burnt after his departure. Wherever he went he erected almshouses, where food and drink were provided free for travellers and poor persons. The laws were very mild, as the people were upright and honourable, and faithful to their oaths and promises. There was no capital punishment; the murderer or robber was not put to death, but driven out of the city and left to wander in the jungle, shunned by his fellowmen, until he died. The taxes were very light, and much of the money was used for education, for rewarding learned men, and for religious purposes. The soil was fertile, and large quantities of grain and fruit were grown. The people lived mostly on wheaten cakes, parched grain, *ghi*, sugar and milk, but men of the warrior caste ate fish and venison also. The cow could not be killed for food. Gold and silver coins and cowrie shells were used for money.

Huien Tsang had come to India principally in order to study, and for this purpose he went to the great Buddhist university at Nalanda in Bihar. It was a handsome building, and there were as many as 10,000 students from all parts of Asia. Some scholars gave up the whole of their lives to learning, and refused honours and rewards of every kind. Many went on with their studies until they were thirty years old, and then, their minds being settled and their education finished, they went into government employment, and the first thing they did was to reward their teachers. The discipline was very strict. For a slight fault, the student was condemned to complete silence for several days. For a grave fault he was expelled, and this was considered a terrible disgrace. Those who were expelled wandered about the roads, and no one would have anything to do with them. At the end of his time, the student was examined by his teachers. If he did well, he was mounted on an elephant covered with precious jewels, and led in triumph round the college. If, on the other hand, he failed to answer the questions put to him, his fellow-students pelted him with mud, and threw him into a ditch. Huien Tsang studied for five years at Nalanda, and once a professor from a rival university challenged him to a public debate. 'If anyone can defeat me,' he said, 'I will give him my head as a proof of his victory.' Huien Tsang overcame him in argument, but he spared his life and made him his disciple.

Huien Tsang was staying as the guest of the king of Assam, when the Emperor heard of his arrival. Harsha was very anxious to meet learned men from all parts of the world. He ordered the Raja of Assam to come at once to his camp, bringing his guest with him. When Huien Tsang arrived at the royal tent, he found the Emperor seated on his throne; by his side was his widowed sister Rajyasri, who was a very learned lady. The Emperor asked Huien Tsang many questions about the doctrine of the Buddha, and was greatly pleased with his answers. Finally, he asked the Master of the Law to accompany him to his capital. Huien Tsang gives an interesting account of the journey. Harsha and the king of Assam travelled on either bank of the Ganges. A vast crowd accompanied them, on foot and in boats, and before them went musicians on elephants, beating drums and sounding trumpets.

The two kings entered the capital dressed to represent the gods Indra and Brahma. They held a canopy over a golden figure of the Buddha, which was carried on a splendid elephant. On arriving at the city they found that a great debating hall had been constructed, with a life-sized image of Buddha. A feast was held, and after it was finished, Huien Tsang explained the Buddhist doctrines to the people assembled there. Many learned men wished to dispute with the Chinese teacher, and some became very angry with him. Thereupon the Emperor proclaimed that if anyone should hurt the Master of the Law in any way, he should be beheaded, and if anyone spoke against him, he should have his tongue cut out. And so, we are told, ' the followers of error withdrew, and there was none to enter the discussion '.

Many of the Hindus were enraged because Harsha was a patron of the Buddhists, and one day they set light to a part of the palace. When the Emperor went to see what had happened, a man rushed out and tried to stab him. Harsha seized the man, and asked him the reason for his act. The man replied that he had been hired by some Brahmins, who had also set fire to the roof of the hall with burning arrows. Five hundred men were arrested, but only the ringleaders were punished. The rest were banished beyond the borders.

On another occasion, Huien Tsang witnessed a great religious festival, known as the Salvation Festival, which was held at Prayaga, the sandy plain at the meeting place of the Ganges and Jumna, where the Khumba Mela is now held every year. Buddhist, Jain and Hindu holy men were invited, together with the poor, the orphans and the bereaved, to receive the royal charity. Vast crowds of people had assembled there. Ten thousand Buddhist monks each received a gold coin, a pearl, and a set of cotton robes. After a month, the Royal Treasury was quite empty, and nothing remained except the horses, elephants and weapons necessary for maintaining order and protecting the Empire. Harsha himself had given away to the poor all his jewels, ornaments and robes, and he had to borrow an old, second-hand garment from his sister Rajyasri.

Harsha's end was a sad one. He sent a Brahmin envoy to his friend the Emperor of China. The Emperor in his turn sent a mandarin to Harsha's court at Thanesar. He was about to return home, loaded with presents, when Harsha was murdered by his minister Arjuna. It was said that the Emperor had fallen under the influence of evil counsellors, and had become cruel and superstitious, but the truth was that the Hindu priests were jealous of the favour he showed to the Buddhists. Huien Tsang says that, during fifty years of his reign, Harsha's face never flushed with anger, and his hands never hurt a living thing. Wild beasts became friendly with men, because no one ever injured them. Harsha was not only a good ruler and a pious man, but he was a learned writer, and was the author of several dramas. He will be remembered, along with Asoka, as one of the best and noblest of the Emperors of ancient India.

AKBAR, THE GREAT MOGUL

JALAL-UD-DIN AKBAR, the greatest of the Mogul Emperors, was born on 23 November, 1542, at the little town of Umarkot in the Sind desert. At that time his father, the Emperor Humayun, was flying from his enemies, the Afghan nobles, who had driven him from his throne. The consequence was that the young prince received very little education. He never learned to read or write; he preferred riding and shooting and playing polo, and he soon found that he possessed a remarkable power of taming wild animals, especially horses and elephants, which nobody else dared to approach. But this does not mean that Akbar was a stupid lad. He had a wonderful memory, and learned by heart long passages from his favourite authors, the mystic Sufi poets, Hafiz and Jalal-ud-din Rumi. He knew a great deal about birds, beasts and plants, and he had a real bent for mechanics. One of his great passions was for art, and he loved painting and music.

Akbar's father remained an exile in Persia and Afghanistan until 1554, when he managed to raise an army and overthrow his rivals. But a short time after his return to Delhi in January 1556 he died from the effects of a fall, and young Akbar, not yet fourteen years old, found himself Emperor of India. His position was a difficult one. The real power was in the hands of his tutor, a powerful nobleman named Bairam Khan, and a clever Hindu of the name of Hemu took the opportunity to stir up a dangerous rebellion. Hemu seized Agra and Delhi, and proclaimed himself as the Raja Vikramaditya, descendant of the ancient Rajput kings. But Bairam Khan defeated him, on 5 November, 1556, at Panipat, on the field where the fortunes of India have been so often decided. Hemu was wounded in the eye by an arrow and brought captive to Akbar. Bairam Khan wished Akbar to put his prisoner to death; but the boy chivalrously refused to do this, and Hemu was killed by his attendants.

For the next four years, Akbar was under the control of Bairam Khan and other courtiers, including his mother and foster-mother, and a son of the latter, named Adham Khan. But after that time he was determined to rule for himself. Bairam Khan was banished. Adham Khan, a brutal and insolent man, he knocked down with a blow of his fist, and ordered the attendants to throw him over the battlements of the palace. He treated his mother with respect and kindness, but warned her never to interfere in politics again. Though Akbar was only eighteen, he realized that he could not rule India without the support of the people. His ancestors had been strangers in the land; he determined to win over the Hindus, especially the gallant Rajputs, who were justly called 'the sword and buckler of Hindustan'. With this in mind, he married, in 1562, a Rajput princess, the daughter of Raja Bihar Mal of Jaipur. After this, nearly all the Rajputs made alliances with him, save the proud Rana of Mewar of the Sisodia clan, who claimed descent from the Sun God himself.

In 1567, Akbar determined to teach the Rana a lesson. In October he laid siege to his capital, the fortress of Chitor. For four months it resisted every assault, but at last Akbar himself managed to kill the brave Rajput commander, Jaimal, with a lucky shot from his musket. After this, the Rajput princesses, headed by the senior Rani, marched in a procession to the underground dungeons beneath, and rather than fall into the hands of the Mussulman conqueror, gave themselves to the flames by the terrible rite known as *jauhar*. Then the garrison threw open the gates, and rushing out, sword in hand, died almost to a man. Chitor was laid waste and remains uninhabited to this day. It is said that a terrible curse rests upon the scene of this tragedy. The gates of the fortress and the kettledrums which used to summon the Rajput clans to war were carried off in triumph to Agra. But the young heir to the throne, Amar Singh, never submitted. He escaped to a remote stronghold in the Rajputana desert, where he held out till his death.

Up to this time, Akbar had spent much of his

time at Agra. But he had no children. At Sikri, about twenty miles away, dwelt the famous saint, Shaikh Salim Chishti, who promised that Akbar should have a son. In August 1569, the Jaipur princess bore him an heir who was named Salim, and afterwards became the Emperor Jahangir. Akbar determined to build himself a new capital on this lucky spot, and he named it Fatehpur Sikri, or the ' City of Victory '. He built here a magnificent tomb of white and black marble, inlaid with mother-of-pearl, in honour of the holy man.

In 1572, Akbar set out to conquer the fertile province of Gujarat. In this campaign, Akbar's life was saved by his gallant Rajput friends, Bhupat Singh and Bhagwan Das. Akbar had pushed ahead with only two hundred horsemen, and after fording a river, he suddenly found himself face to face with a much larger force of hostile cavalry. The Emperor gave the order to charge, and a hand-to-hand fight followed, in very difficult country, cut up by steep banks, narrow lanes and thick cactus hedges. Akbar was attacked by three of the enemy, and might well have been killed; but Bhagwan Das sent a spear-thrust through the leading man, while Bhupat Singh drove off the other two. Meanwhile, the main body had come up and the enemy was routed; but Bhupat Singh lost his life. The Sultan Muzaffar III fled, and was caught hiding in a field. The rich city of Ahmedabad opened its gates, and the ports of Cambay and Surat were taken. This gave Akbar a much needed outlet to the Arabian Sea, and greatly increased the trade and prosperity of his lands. Surat was very important, as it was the chief port from which Muslims sailed when they were going on the Haj pilgrimage to Mecca.

In the following year, in the middle of the hot weather, Gujarat rebelled, and the Imperial garrison at Ahmedabad was closely besieged. In spite of the heat, Akbar, with a tiny force of 3,000 horsemen, raced across the Rajputana desert, covering six hundred miles in eleven days. The rebels were taken completely by suprise and fled in such a panic, as it was said, that their opponents ' pulled the arrows out of the quivers on their backs, and used their own weapons against them '. Akbar charged ' like a tiger ' at the head of his men, and when his horse was shot under him, he mounted another. The rebellion was stamped out, and Gujarat needed no third lesson.

On his return, Akbar commemorated his victory by erecting at Fatehpur Sikri a noble gateway of red sandstone known as the Buland Darawaza, which is one of the most striking monuments in the whole of India. Around the doorway are two inscriptions. One recounts the Emperor's achievements; the other reads,

> Jesus Son of Mary says, ' *The world is a bridge ; pass over it, but build no house upon it.*'

In 1574, Akbar rounded off his conquests by **overrunning** Bengal. He was now master of the whole of Hindustan from the Bay of Bengal to the Arabian Sea.

But Akbar was no mere conqueror. He determined that his Empire should be organized on the best possible lines. He divided it into twelve provinces, each ruled by a Subadar or Governor, who was always a member of the Royal family. Under the Subadar were Mansabdars or officials who were classified according to the number of horsemen they contributed to the Imperial Army. The Mansabdar was both a military and a civil officer. He was responsible for maintaining law and order, and collecting the revenue. He also tried criminal cases: civil disputes were settled by the Kazi or judge. Towns were governed by an officer known as the Kotwal. The Emperor took care that none of the offices under the Crown should become hereditary. He could remove at will and punish any of the officials who abused his powers. The Emperor was assisted in his work by four Ministers, and every day he appeared at the *Jharoka* or Window of Audience, where he received petitions from any of his subjects, high or low, who had suffered any grievance or wrong.

The chief source of revenue in India has always been the land. In order to prevent the peasants from being unjustly taxed, Akbar employed Todar Mal, a clever Hindu from Oudh. Todar Mal carried out a survey of all the land in the Empire, and made an assessment of the amount to be paid. This was based on the area, the nature of the crop, and the fertility of the soil; the amount to be paid was calculated at one-third of the average produce, and had to be rendered in cash. Thus the farmers knew exactly what they had to pay, and extortion on the part of the officials was well nigh impossible. A number of dues vexatious to Hindus were abolished, including the *jizya* or poll tax on non-Muslims, and the tax on pilgrims going to the great Hindu shrines such as Jaganath in Orissa.

One of the chief causes of trouble in India has always been the question of religion. In the past, there had been teachers like Nanak and Kabir who tried to find something in common between Hinduism and Islam. The Sufi poets, on whom Akbar had been brought up, taught that different religions are only various ways of worshipping the One God. Akbar must also have learnt a great deal about Hinduism from his Rajput wives and friends. His ambition had always been to bring to a state of real unity the vast empire over which he ruled.

Akbar therefore assembled together learned men of all religions in a great hall, known as the Ibadat Khana or Hall of Worship, where they were to explain their beliefs. There were doctors of the Islamic sects, a Parsee High Priest from Surat named Dastur Meherji Rana, a Jain teacher named Hiravijaya, and two Jesuit missionaries from Goa. The coming of the latter was a very important event in the Emperor's life. The population of the capital was amazed to see these simple priests, clad in plain black, amid the Mogul courtiers, resplendent in their silken robes and gorgeous jewels. Akbar received them kindly, and accepted as a present a copy of the Bible printed in four languages.

The Emperor became greatly attached to his Jesuit friends, and gave them many privileges. He allowed them to build a chapel, and even entrusted them with the education of his son Murad. He spent night after night with them, questioning and debating. On the other hand, the Fathers learnt Persian, and were soon able to translate the Gospels and dispute with the Muslim religious leaders in their own tongue. But the Emperor was never converted to Christianity, though he expressed the profoundest admiration for the life and teaching of Jesus Christ. 'He had the Spirit of God, and neither man nor angel spoke as He spoke,' was one of Akbar's characteristic sayings.

Finally, in 1582, Akbar proclaimed his own creed, which he named the *Din Ilahi*, or Divine Faith. It combined what the Emperor thought to be the essential principles of Christianity, Jainism, Hinduism and Zoroastrianism; in the words of Abul Fazl, 'it had the great advantage of not losing what was good in one religion, while gaining whatever was better in the other. In this way honour would be rendered to God, peace would be given to the people, and security to the Empire'. The Emperor came to be regarded by the followers of his new Faith as a semi-divine being, and their spiritual guide. Akbar's great experiment did not succeed. The religion which was to have united all, pleased none, and it attracted few outside the royal circle.

Akbar was a great patron of the arts. He was particularly interested in painting. He employed two famous Hindu artists, Daswanath and Basawan, whose works are still treasured by connoisseurs. A whole army of calligraphers was kept at work writing and illuminating the *Akbar Nama*, or chronicle of the Emperor's life, composed by Abul Fazl, and adorning it with illustrations. Translations were made of the Hindu scriptures, that of the *Bhagavad Gita* being the work of Faizi, the poet laureate. At the time of his death, Akbar had a library of 24,000 illuminated manuscripts, valued at many hundreds of thousands of rupees.

Among the foreign visitors to the Court was one little party which passed almost unnoticed at the time. This consisted of three Englishmen, John Newbery, William Leedes and Ralph Fitch, who bore a letter from Queen Elizabeth. They reached the capital in 1585, after many strange adventures.

The Queen's letter requested that they might be 'honestly intreated and received', in order to start trading operations, 'by which means the mutual and friendly traffic of merchandise on both sides might come'.

The Englishmen were greatly impressed by the

prosperity of the country and the splendour of the buildings of Agra, in comparison with which London appeared like a tiny village. In the bazaars there was 'a great resort of merchandize from Persia and out of India and very much merchandize of silk and cloth and precious stones, both rubies, diamonds and pearls'. Apparently Elizabeth's letter was not considered worthy of a reply: Akbar, if he had heard of the English at all, was probably told by his Portuguese friends that they were a tiny nation inhabiting a distant island in the far north, and quite beneath his notice! It was not till the succeeding reign that the English succeeded in getting permission to start a trading factory at the port of Surat. Leedes obtained a post as a court jeweller, and settled down in the country. Newbery attempted to return by the overland route and disappeared. Only Fitch reached home, after eight years' travel, in the course of which he visited Bengal, Burma and the Malay peninsula. His account of what he had seen led to the foundation of the East India Company.

Meanwhile the Emperor, ever restless and ambitious, was pursuing a series of campaigns, the aim of which was to round off his conquests. In 1581, he learned that his cousin, Mohammed Hakim, had raised the standard of revolt in Kabul, and he hastened to the spot. The mighty host, with its elephants, cavalry and mounted archers, moved forward to the beat of a great drum. The day's march was carefully measured, and every night an encampment was laid out. In the midst was the Royal Pavilion, painted white and visible for miles around. A long wait followed on the banks of the Indus, while the engineers were busy constructing a bridge of boats over that mighty river, now swollen by violent storms. Soon Peshawar was reached. The next obstacle was the Khyber Pass, through which the engineers had to construct a road; but Akbar's energy overcame every difficulty, and he was soon knocking at the gates of Kabul. Mohammed Hakim thereupon surrendered.

In 1588, trouble again broke out in the Punjab, and Akbar left Fatehpur Sikri, this time for ever. He made his headquarters in Lahore, and from that centre he undertook the conquest of Sind, which gave him command of the mouth of the river Indus. Soon after, he conquered the beautiful vale of Kashmir, which his successor adorned with pleasure gardens now famous throughout the world. Baluchistan and Kandahar were annexed, and only the Deccan remained for him to conquer in order that he might be Padshah of the mightiest Empire in the world. In the Deccan were the independent Muhammadan kingdoms of Ahmednagar and Bijapur, neither of which was willing to acknowledge the Mogul from the north. Ahmednagar was defended by the queen regent, Chand Bibi, who fought at the head of her men in shining armour, her face covered by a silken veil. But in 1600, the plucky queen was killed in a local rising and Ahmednagar surrendered. There remained, however, the mighty fortress of Asirgarh in Khandesh, the 'Gibraltar of the East', rising out of the plain to a height of nine hundred feet, with its sheer precipices and its triple lines of walls. It was said to have stocks of food and water sufficient to last for ten years. The commandant, an Abyssinian by birth, was old and blind, but a man of great valour. For a year, Abul Fazl carried on the siege with little effect. At length some of the officers of the garrison were corrupted by bribes, and the gates were opened.

The last years of the great Emperor's life were clouded with sorrow. Devoted friends died or were killed in battle, and his children caused him great trouble. His beloved son and heir, Salim, even rebelled against his father, and advanced on Agra with thirty thousand horsemen. Abul Fazl was ordered to bring the young prince to his senses; but Salim hired a ruffian named Bir Singh, who waylaid Abul Fazl and his escort and put them to the sword. Akbar never recovered from the death of the oldest and dearest of his friends. Father and son were afterwards reconciled, but the Emperor was prostrated by the shock. On 22 October, 1605, he fell ill with dysentery. He was only fifty-two, but he was worn out by a life of toil and exertion. Very soon he was too ill to speak; but he made signs to Salim to gird himself with the sword of Humayun, and placed the imperial turban on his head. He died five days later and the funeral was of the simplest. A gap was broken in the palace walls, and through it the body of the great ruler was carried on the shoulders of Salim and his son Khusru.

Akbar lived in an era of mighty statesmen, Shah Abbas of Persia, Philip II of Spain, Henry IV of France and Elizabeth of England, but in many respects he was head and shoulders above them all. 'He was a born king of men, with a rightful claim to rank as one of the greatest monarchs of history. That claim rests securely on the basis of his extraordinary natural gifts and magnificent attainments.'

SIVAJI THE MARATHA

IF you make a journey from Bombay to Poona, you will travel up what are known as the Ghats, a great range of mountains running parallel to the sea, through a wild country covered with jungle, with here and there an ancient fort overlooking the neighbourhood from a rocky height. Finally you will come to a broad plain, stretching for many miles across Central India. This is the Deccan or Maharashtra, the home of the Marathas.

In the seventeenth century, the Marathas were, as they are now, simple and hardy folk, intensely fond of their fields, but when the occasion arose, brave and skilful fighting men. They formed a number of clans, ruled over by chieftains who claimed to be of Rajput descent. At that time, most of the surrounding country was part of the Muhammadan kingdom of Ahmednagar. Many of the chieftains were in the service of the Ahmednagar kings, and among them was a certain Shahji Bhonsle. He was married to a lady of ancient family named Jijabai, and in May 1627, while Shahji was away in Southern India on a military expedition, his son Sivaji was born at the hill fortress of Shivner. Jijabai was a pious Hindu, and she employed as a tutor for her boy a Brahmin of the name of Dadoji Dondadev. Though he showed little interest in reading or writing, the lad eagerly listened to the ancient stories from the Ramayana and the Mahabharata. He loved to hear of the deeds of the Pandava brothers, of the hero-god Rama and his faithful wife the princess Sita, and their adventures with the demon Ravana. The young Sivaji spent much of his time in the company of the Mavalis, the local hillmen who knew every inch of the country, and who taught him to ride, to shoot with the bow, and to track the wild beast to its lair.

Sivaji thus learnt to love freedom and to hate the idea of a life of luxury as a nobleman at one of the Muslim courts. Above all, he became more and more determined to free his country from Muhammadan rule, and to re-establish the old Hindu Raj. In 1649, when he was only nineteen, he gathered together a small body of followers, and seized the fortress of Torna. Soon after, he managed to pounce upon a convoy of treasure going to the Muhammadan governor of Kalayan, and this gave him the money he so sorely needed for his plans. The Sultan of Bijapur was so angry when he heard about this, that he took Shahji and shut him up in a tiny cell, which he threatened to build up entirely unless Sivaji ceased to stir up trouble in the Deccan. Shahji was released after a time, but Sivaji began to rebel once more, and the Sultan of Bijapur sent an army to capture him.

The Bijapur army was under the command of a

general named Afzal Khan. Afzal Khan set out for the Deccan in September 1659, and he boasted that he would quickly bring back the 'mountain rat' in chains to the Sultan's court. As he marched through the Deccan, Afzal Khan destroyed a number of shrines sacred to the Hindus. Among them were those of the god Vithoba of Pandharpur, dear to all Marathas, and of Amba Bhavani, the goddess of the Bhonsle family. This aroused great indignation, and Sivaji's followers vowed that they would fight to their last drop of blood in order to repel the invader. As the Bijapur army advanced, Sivaji and his small body of men fell back before them through the dense jungle, towards the stronghold of Pratapgarh, which he had built on a rock in a very wild part of the country, not very far from the present hill station of Mahableshwar. Afzal Khan began to be alarmed when he found himself in this wild land, destitute of proper roads, where he was constantly attacked by the Marathas. He therefore made a plan to ask Sivaji to a conference and then arrest him. When Sivaji heard about this, he determined to outwit his enemy. He agreed that a meeting should be held in an open spot not far from Pratapgarh, and here he erected a handsome tent. In the surrounding woods he placed strong bodies of Marathas in ambush, ready to fall upon the foe at the given signal, which was to be the firing of a gun from the walls of the fortress.

Sivaji spent the night in prayer to the goddess

Amba Bhavani. In the morning, he knelt before his mother and asked her blessing. Under his white robe he wore armour; on his left hand was a terrible weapon, the *Vaghnakh*, or tiger's claws of steel, and at his side hung his trusty Bhavani sword. Afzal Khan came with a few followers and Sivaji went to meet him. When they embraced, Afzal Khan seized Sivaji and tried to drag him away, but Sivaji stabbed him with the tiger's claws and drew his sword and cut him down. At that moment, as had been arranged, a shot rang out from the fortress above, and the Marathas, rushing out from their hiding places, took the Bijapuris completely by surprise. The Muhammadans fled in all directions, and vast spoils, arms, cannon, horses, saddles and money were captured. Sivaji at once stopped the slaughter. He told his men to spare their prisoners. Those who were wounded were well cared for and sent home, each with fresh clothes and a small sum of money.

Sivaji's victory not only gave him the arms and munitions which he so urgently needed, but it brought him great fame. The Marathas began to regard him as their national hero, and thousands joined his army. The Bijapur government sent fresh troops to catch him, and at one time he was besieged in the fortress of Panhala. But he slipped out in the night, and when the Muhammadans pursued him very closely, a gallant officer named Baji Prabhu held the narrow pass at Rangana at the cost of his life, until Sivaji had got safely away.

Soon after this, Sivaji built himself a magnificent fortress at Raigarh, which became his capital. Here the Marathas retired after their plundering expeditions. It soon contained vast quantities of loot, gold mohurs, Spanish dollars, bars of gold, diamonds and pearls and silks, a great armoury and ample stores.

Soon after this Sivaji made peace with Bijapur, but now he found that he had to face a far more dangerous and crafty foe. The Emperor Aurangzeb was determined to conquer the Deccan, and he sent a great army under his uncle Shayista Khan for this purpose. The Marathas gave the Moguls no peace. Every night they swarmed round the baggage, carrying off horses, camels and men, and killing the camp followers. Shayista Khan took up his quarters in Poona, and one night Sivaji and a few bold followers entered the city in a wedding procession. In the middle of the night they suddenly raided Shayista Khan's palace, killing everyone they met. The Mogul general jumped out of his bedroom window, and only just escaped alive. One of Sivaji's followers cut off the general's fingers with his sword. In 1664, Sivaji marched right across Gujarat, and surprised the great port of Surat. The Marathas overran the town, but when they came to the English trading factory they were beaten off. This was the first occasion on which the Marathas came into contact with the English. Sivaji would not allow his troops to harm the Christian missionaries, because, as he said, 'These *Padres* are good men'. The Moguls sent an army to relieve Surat, but long before it arrived, the Marathas vanished as quickly as they had come, taking with them great quantities of rupees in booty and vast spoils.

It proved impossible for Sivaji to hold out for very long against the mighty Mogul armies, and at length he was persuaded by Raja Jai Singh, a powerful Rajput nobleman in the service of the Emperor, to visit Agra and come to terms with Aurangzeb. But when Sivaji arrived at the Mogul capital, he realized that he had been misled. At the Imperial darbar which was held every morning in the Hall of Audience, he was only given a very inferior rank. When he returned to the house which had been assigned to him, he found himself practically a prisoner. Guards were set at the doors, and he was unable to leave. So a plot was made with the aid of his captain Tanaji Malusre. Sivaji had been in the habit of sending huge baskets of sweetmeats to be distributed among the poor. One day it was announced that the Maratha leader was ill with a severe fever. The guard looked into his bedroom, and Sivaji appeared to be asleep there covered with a blanket. But really it was not Sivaji at all, but Hiraji Pharjand, a faithful follower who had consented to take his place. Sivaji and his son Sambhaji had been carried out of the town in the sweetmeat baskets; horses had been got ready, and they were riding as hard as they could for Mathura.

Mathura is a sacred Hindu city, always crowded with pilgrims, *bairagis*, and other holy men. Here Tanaji was waiting for him. Sivaji shaved his beard, stripped off his silken robes, smeared his body with ashes, and soon lost himself in the crowd. His son went with him as his *chela* or disciple. Presently they joined a crowd of pilgrims going to Prayaga or Allahabad, another holy place. From Allahabad, Sivaji went on to Benares, and by this time the Mogul officials had given up looking for him. Slowly he wandered back to the Deccan. One day, as the Princess Jijabai was sitting in the room of her apartments in the castle of Raigarh, looking out on the Deccan and mourning for her lost son, a servant came and said that a holy man was waiting outside. The princess received him, and he fell at her feet. When she asked his business, he stripped off his disguise, and stood before her. It was Sivaji himself!

The news of the return of their hero spread like fire all over the Deccan, and great were the rejoicings among the Marathas. But much work remained to be done. The stronghold of Kondana, overlooking Poona, was still in Mogul hands, and it is said that Jijabai swore an oath not to eat bread or drink water until it was captured. The exploit was entrusted to Tanaji Malusre, popularly known as the Lion, the oldest and bravest of Sivaji's comrades in arms. The undertaking was a desperate one. The fort lies on a flat-topped rock, with sheer precipices fifty feet high on every side. It is crowned by a strong wall, with towers at intervals. The only approach leads to a huge gate, studded with iron nails and securely barred. The garrison consisted of a thousand picked men under a brave Rajput officer, Udai Ban.

Tanaji and a few chosen companions set out on a dark, moonless night in February 1670. It was very cold, and the sentries, huddled up in their cloaks, were not keeping good watch. Within, everyone was making merry, for Udai Ban and his officers thought that they were quite safe. The Marathas crept up to the foot of the rock, and a Mavali managed to climb up and let down a rope-ladder. One by one Tanaji and three hundred Marathas ascended, while the remainder went round to the gateway. The nearest sentry was shot by an arrow, and the Marathas leaped over the wall. Some rushed in and threw open the gate for the rest to enter. By this time, the garrison was aroused, and torches flashed on the shields of the men as they hurriedly assembled. Immediately Tanaji gave the order to charge, and the air was filled with wild cries of *Din! Din!* and *Har, Har, Mahadev!* as the two forces met in fierce combat. Quarter was neither given nor taken; Tanaji fell at the head of his men, slain, it is said, in single combat with Udai Ban. The rest of the garrison was put to the sword, save five hundred badly wounded Rajputs who were made prisoners; others hurled themselves over the battlements rather than surrender. Then the victors fired a building to signal the news to the anxious watchers on the walls of Raigarh. But Sivaji was broken-hearted at the death of his old comrade in arms. 'I have won my fort and lost my Lion', he said sadly; and the stronghold is known to this day as Singarh, 'the Lion's Fort'.

Sivaji was now at last the ruler of the Deccan, and it was necessary that he should be crowned. It was three hundred and fifty years since the last Hindu king had been overthrown by the Muhammadan invaders, and the whole Maratha nation was longing for the restoration of the Hindu Raj. In May 1674, preparations were begun at Raigarh for the great event. Gaga Bhat, a famous scholar, was fetched all the way from Benares, and he brought with him water from the sacred Ganges for the purpose. Eleven thousand Brahmins, with their wives and children, were fed at the Raja's expense, and ambassadors from the surrounding states flocked in; among them was an Englishman, George Oxenden, the representative of the English factory at Surat.

The Raja was weighed against gold, which was distributed among the poor in atonement for his sins. Clad in pure white silk and garlanded with flowers, he sat on a golden stool, with his son Sambhaji on one side and his consort Soyrabai on the other, while the Brahmins chanted the sacred *mantras* and sprinkled him with Ganges water from golden ewers. Then the Raja changed into his kingly robes, placed the royal turban on his head, and, girding the Bhavani sword at his side, went in procession to the throne room. As he mounted the throne, Gaga Bhat raised the golden umbrella over his head, and greeted him with the words, 'Hail, Sivaji Maharaja Chhatrapati!' The immense crowd took up the cry, 'Victory, Victory to Shiva raja!' The trumpets sounded, and the artillery fired salvo after salvo. From one fortress to the other, for hundreds of miles right down to the distant Konkan, the glad news was passed, and thundering cannon announced to the waiting people that once again they had a Hindu ruler.

Sivaji's last expedition was undertaken in 1676. He marched into the Carnatic with a great army, where the kingdom of Bijapur was at its last gasp. The strong fortress of Jinji surrendered; Vellore was taken, together with the Kolar and Bangalore districts. Four years later, while he was carrying all before him, the great warrior died, from what at first had seemed a trifling injury, at Raigarh, in the fifty-third year of his age. He had made the Marathas rulers of the Deccan, the Konkan and the Carnatic, from the Vindhya mountains to Cape Comorin. Above all, he was the man who started the downfall of the Mogul Empire. The 'mountain rat' gnawed through the supports which upheld that mighty structure, though he left it to his successors to complete its overthrow.

Sivaji was a strict disciplinarian; no woman was admitted to his camp on pain of death, and all plunder had to be surrendered for fair division.

He was not only a great soldier, but a great administrator. He saw that people of every caste, Brahmin, Prabhu, Maratha and Mahar, had their proper duties and privileges. He was no despot, and was assisted in the work of government by a Council of Eight Ministers, headed by the Peshwa or Prime Minister. The power of the local nobles over the peasants was checked, and the amount of money to be taken as land revenue was fairly assessed.

In appearance, Sivaji was tall and slight, with long arms, a fair complexion and a beard worn in Mussulman fashion. He had piercing eyes and a resolute face, handsome and intelligent. His manner was frank and pleasing. He was chivalrous to his foes, though he showed no mercy to traitors. Above all, he was a sincerely religious man, respecting the beliefs of others. He took no important step without praying to his goddess Bhavani, and often spent hours at her shrine. He owed much to the teaching of his old Brahmin tutor Dadoji Dondadev, and above all, to his mother Jijabai, a typical Hindu woman. After his coronation, he gave his whole kingdom as a gift to God into the hands of his teacher Ramdas, who returned it to him as a sacred trust.

Such a man was Sivaji Bhonsle, the founder of the Maratha Empire, and one of the greatest Hindus of all time.

MAHARAJA RANJIT SINGH

THE story of the rise of the Sikhs is an interesting one. Originally they were members of a sect founded by Nanak, their first Guru or spiritual teacher. Nanak tried to found a religion which would be acceptable to both Hindus and Muhammadans. When he was dying in 1538, his followers quarrelled because they were doubtful whether to bury his body with Muslim rites, or burn him as a Hindu. Nanak said, ' Let the Hindus heap up flowers on my right hand, and the Muslims on my left. Those whose flowers are fresh in the morning may have my body '. In the morning, both heaps of flowers were bright and fresh, but the Guru's body had vanished.

Time went on, and the Sikhs or disciples increased in numbers, until they became a powerful body. Arjun, the fifth Guru, built the Golden Temple at Amritsar, and put together the Adi Granth, or Sikh Bible, which consists of the sayings of the Gurus. Arjun was executed by the Emperor Jahangir, and after this, the Sikhs became a martial race, pledged to make war on the Mogul Empire. Hargobind, Arjun's successor, declared, ' My necklace shall be my sword-belt, and my turban shall be adorned with the royal aigrette'. Teg Bahadur, the ninth Guru, was put to death by the Emperor Aurangzeb in 1675, because he would not embrace Islam. Before his death he said, 'Emperor Aurangzeb, I was on the top story of my prison, but I was not looking at thy private apartments, nor thy Queen's. I was looking in in the direction of the Europeans, who are coming from beyond the seas to tear down thy *purdahs*[1] and destroy thy empire'.

Govind Singh, the tenth and last Guru, formed the Sikhs into a brotherhood, known as the Khalsa or Pure Ones. They took the name Singh, a Lion. They gave up wine and tobacco, and wore the five articles beginning with the letter *k*, long hair, short drawers, an iron discus or bangle, a dagger and a comb. After Govind Singh's death, the war against the Moguls was carried on by a leader named Banda, who did great damage until he was caught and executed. The bravery of the Sikhs is shown by a story told by a Muhammadan historian. A mother had obtained from the Emperor a pardon for her son. She arrived just as the executioner was raising his sword. But the boy cried out, 'My mother is telling falsehoods. With all my heart I join the Sikhs in devotion to the Guru. Send me quickly after my companions.'

In the eighteenth century the Punjab was in a state of confusion. The Mogul Empire had broken up, and all order was lost. The country was

[1] Purdah, a curtain serving to screen women from the sight of strangers.

ravaged by Marathas from the South and Afghans from the North. The only law was that of the sword. The Sikhs were divided into twelve *misls* or clans, each at war with the other. The most powerful clan was that of the Sukarchakias, who were constantly at war with their neighbours, the Bhangis. The head of the Sukarchakias was Raja Mohan Singh, and in 1780 a son was born to him and named Ranjit Singh. Ranjit Singh was brought up as a soldier from childhood. At the age of ten, he saw his first battle, seated on his war elephant in a *howdah* beside his father. One of the enemy climbed into the *howdah* and tried to kill the boy, but was cut down. In 1792 at the age of twelve he succeeded his father, and soon after he was nearly drowned in a flood which swept away his camp, with many horses and camels. Like the Emperor Akbar at an earlier date, he had first to rid himself of the ' petticoat government ' of his mother and his mother-in-law, fierce ladies who led their armies in person. They were both defeated and locked up in fortresses.

Ranjit Singh was now master of his own house, and a lucky accident made him very powerful. Shah Zaman, the Afghan ruler, had invaded the Punjab, and lost twelve of his precious cannon in a rising of the waters of the Jhelum river. Ranjit Singh rescued the guns, and gave them back on the condition that he was recognized as ruler of Lahore, the capital of the Punjab. Shortly after, he attacked Amritsar, the Sacred City of the Sikhs.

Amritsar was in the hands of the Bhangis, his rivals, who also owned the famous Zam Zam gun, cast from the copper waterpots taken from the Hindus by the Muslims as *jizya* or poll tax. Ranjit Singh had a passion for guns. It was said that if he learnt that there was a gun in a fort, he could not rest until he had taken the fort to get the gun, or until the gun had been given up to save the fort. Amritsar soon fell, and the Zam Zam gun became Ranjit Singh's property. To-day it stands outside the Lahore Museum.

There were certain states each of the Sutlej to which both Ranjit Singh and the English laid claim. In 1806, Ranjit Singh crossed the Sutlej, and for a time it looked as though this action would lead to war. But the Viceroy, Lord Minto, sent a clever young political officer named Charles Metcalfe to arrange matters. Metcalfe agreed that the Sutlej should be the boundary between the two powers. He had as his bodyguard two companies of Indian infantry. These were on one occasion attacked by a large mob of fanatics, known as Akalis, but owing to good discipline they easily beat them off. This fact greatly impressed Ranjit Singh. So far, the Sikhs had despised infantry, and all their troops were mounted men.

Now Ranjit Singh saw that the real power in battle lay in well-drilled infantry and artillery. He obtained the services of two French officers, Generals Ventura and Allard, who had fought under Napoleon and afterwards had taken service under the Shah of Persia, and several other Europeans including an Irish artillery officer named Gardner. Between them, they built up the Army of the Khalsa, consisting of thirty thousand infantry with three hundred guns. These troops, like Europeans, had red uniforms and regular pay. Ranjit Singh himself wore a similar uniform, and learnt to drill and command his troops like a European general. The cavalry on the other hand kept their many-coloured silks, their armour, swords, old fashioned guns, and small, round shields.

Very soon, Ranjit Singh found a chance to try out his new army. The great fortified city of Multan was held by an Afghan governor, Nawab Muzaffar Khan, who refused to pay tribute. In January 1818, Ranjit Singh laid siege to Multan. He brought up the Zam Zam gun to batter the walls with its huge stone cannon balls. But as fast as a breach was made, it was filled up by the besieged, and the storming parties were driven back. The siege went on for month after month. At last a band of Akalis seized a bastion, and the troops poured in. But the Nawab, an Afghan noble of ancient family, with his eight sons, refused to surrender. Drawing their swords, they stood with their backs to the wall. Muzaffar Khan had a long white beard, and was a noble figure. ' Come on,' he cried to his enemies, ' and let us perish like men.' But the Sikhs preferred to pick them off with their matchlocks at a safe distance.

When the old man and five of his sons had fallen, the remaining three surrendered. Ranjit Singh got two crores of rupees in booty from Multan.

Soon after, Ranjit Singh undertook another notable exploit. This was the conquest of the beautiful valley of Kashmir. It was a very difficult undertaking, because the Sikhs were unused to mountain warfare, and were constantly harassed by the Pathans and other tribesmen. At first, the Afghans promised to help the Sikhs, but after a while they quarrelled. The Sikhs then seized the fortress of Attock, which commanded the chief crossing over the river Indus. On 13 July, 1813, the Afghans, led by Prince Dost Mohammed Khan, broke the Sikh line of battle by a brilliant cavalry charge, but in the end he was beaten by General Diwan Mokham Chand. In the following year, the Sikh army had to retreat from Kashmir, and was caught in the mountain passes by the bursting of the monsoon. Many soldiers were swept away by the floods and perished. The country was not subdued until 1823, after which Ranjit Singh laid siege to the Afghan town of Peshawar. Peshawar was held by a general named Yar Mahommed Khan, who owned an Arab mare called Laili. Ranjit Singh was very fond of horses, and Laili was said to be the most beautiful mare in Asia. She was grey, with black points, and was sixteen hands high. The Afghan general was arrested and told that he would stay in prison until she was given up. After she was taken, she lived in a silver stall, with gold bangles round her fetlocks. Ranjit Singh said that she cost him sixty lakhs of rupees and 1,200 good soldiers!

Ranjit Singh was now master of the whole of the Punjab and Kashmir. He built himself a fine capital at Lahore, the old Mogul headquarters. Many Europeans visited his Court and had a ready welcome. Among them were Baron Carl Von Hugel, the German scientist, Victor de Jacquemont, the French traveller, and Moorcroft, the English explorer who afterwards perished in the Hindu Kush mountains. Although Ranjit Singh, like Akbar and Sivaji, had had little education, he was of a very enquiring mind, and liked to meet learned men of all nationalities.

The country was well governed, though strict measures had to be used to keep order among the wild tribesmen on the border. Raja Dina Nath, a Rajput, was Finance Minister, and he saw that the peasants were not overtaxed by the Sikh nobles. Lehna Singh, a Sikh, was Master of Ordnance, and was responsible for casting and founding the great guns which formed the chief part of Ranjit Singh's artillery. The Army, as we have seen, was commanded by European generals. The Prime Minister was Fakir Aziz-ud-din, from Bokhara, a physician by profession. He belonged to the Sufi sect, and when he was asked whether he was a Muhammadan or a Sikh by religion, he answered, 'I am like a man floating on a mighty river. I turn my eyes to the land, but I cannot distinguish either bank.' He was a good Persian and Arabic scholar, and kept a college at his own expense. By thus skilfully mixing together men of various creeds and nationalities, Ranjit Singh evaded all attempts at plotting against his power.

Ranjit Singh did not altogether like the advance of the English to his borders. By this time they had overthrown the Marathas, who had been the leading power after the fall of the Mogul Empire, and when he looked at the map of India, he exclaimed, *Sab lal hojayega*, ' Soon it will all be red!' But he was too prudent to quarrel with them. In 1831, the Governor General, Lord Bentinck, met him at a place called Rupar. The English were very much afraid that the Russians would seize Afghanistan, and they wanted the Sikhs to be a buffer-state. There was a grand Darbar, and the Sikh army was drawn up on parade. The regular infantry, in their scarlet coats, looked like a solid red wall. Behind these were the tribal leaders with the irregular cavalry, fierce horsemen in coats of mail, with shields inlaid with gold and heron-plumes in their helmets. Maharaja's bodyguard was clad in gay coloured silks, but Ranjit Singh himself was dressed in a plain suit of white. For days the two armies entertained one another with sports and feasting. Tourneys were held, and the Maharaja, in spite of being paralysed, amazed everyone by his superb horsemanship. Seven years later, another Governor General, Lord Auckland, also visited him. Lord

Auckland's sister, Miss Eden, says that the Maharaja, with his red coat lined with squirrel's fur and his long grey beard, looked like a little old mouse. It was hard, she said, to believe that the small, tottering, one-eyed man ruled an Empire containing the fiercest and most martial tribes in all India. In June 1839, he died; shortly before his death, he bestowed his jewels and horses on various Sikh shrines, and two Ranis accompanied him to the funeral pyre.

Ranjit Singh was the leading Indian ruler of his day. He found the Sikhs split up into a number of warring clans; he left them a mighty Empire. He was a splendid soldier, and was often compared by European travellers to Bonaparte himself. He introduced peace and order where it had been unknown for centuries, and himself toured from one end of his kingdom to the other, in order to see that his orders were being obeyed. In appearance he was ugly, with only one eye, a face disfigured by smallpox, and his lower limbs paralysed. Only on horseback did he appear the man he really was. But although feeble, blind and paralysed, he kept his fierce chiefs in subjection, and to the last day of his life his orders were instantly obeyed. His personality overawed all who came near him. His Minister was asked in which eye Ranjit Singh was blind. 'The splendour of his face is such,' replied Aziz-ud-din, 'that I have never dared to look close enough to discover that.'

SIR SAIYID AHMED KHAN

Sir Saiyid Ahmed Khan is perhaps the greatest Muhammadan India has produced since the English became rulers of the country. His family came from Herat to Delhi, and his grandfather was an army commander under the Emperor Alamgir II. Saiyid Ahmed was born in October 1817. At that time, nearly all power had passed to the East India Company, but the Mogul Emperors still maintained their splendour and pomp. The lad spent much of his early life in the Court at Delhi, and was soundly educated by his mother, a pious and learned lady. Like all other Muslim boys he was taught the Quran, and besides this, he studied Arabic and Persian literature. He learned to love especially the Persian poets of the Sufi sect, and from them he took the enlightened ideas about religion which were such a feature of his later life.

In 1836, his father died, and Saiyid Ahmed, finding little for an ambitious young man to do in the Court of Delhi, determined to enter the British service, though his family were opposed to the step. He probably foresaw that the Mogul power was fast coming to an end, and that the British

Government was taking its place. He was made a Sheristidar, or Court Reader, and did so well that he quickly rose to the rank of Munsif or sub-judge. In 1844 he published an interesting and learned work in Urdu, about the various ruined cities around Delhi, and the famous poets and saints who had flourished there.

Some years later, Saiyid Ahmed Khan became Munsif of Bijnaur, a town of about 13,000 people, between Meerut and Roorkee. He still held this post, when, in 1857, the Indian Mutiny broke out. The sepoys of the Bengal Army rose and murdered their officers, and soon all appearance of law and order was lost. Some Rohillas came and plundered the town, and wished to throw open the jail. There were eight European officers, four ladies and a number of children in the cantonment. Saiyid Ahmed Khan and the Deputy Collector, Rehmat Khan, worked magnificently in order to rescue them. In the end Saiyid Ahmed Khan succeeded in persuading the Rohilla chief to let the Europeans go safely to Meerut.

Meanwhile, Saiyid Ali Khan's family was in Delhi, which was being besieged by the British troops. When the city was taken by storm, his uncle and cousin, most unfortunately, were killed; while his mother found shelter in the house of a servant. Saiyid Ahmed Khan went to Delhi with all speed, and brought his mother to Meerut. But she was so much shaken by the experiences which she had undergone during the siege, that she died of shock about a month later. Saiyid Ahmed Khan stuck to his post until the rising was finally put down, and did all in his power to help the Government.

Mr. Shakespeare, the Collector of the district, speaking of the work that Saiyid Ahmed Khan and his companions did at the time, said, ' I cannot exaggerate the help they affoided me during this period of incessant anxiety and danger. On every occasion of special anxiety and difficulty, such as when the jail broke and I found it advisable to throw the Treasure down the well, the officers in question were ever ready, and behaved with great discretion and courage '.

Sir John Strachey, afterwards Finance Minister to the Government of India, said that no man ever gave nobler proofs of conspicuous courage and loyalty. ' No language which I could use ', he declared, ' would be worthy of the devotion he showed.' For this work the Government presented Saiyid Ahmed Khan with a *khillat* and sword of Honour.

Saiyid Ahmed Khan afterwards published a book on the Indian Mutiny, in which he analysed the causes of that terrible tragedy. The real reason, he wrote, was that the Government of India was out of touch with the people, and did not know what the masses were thinking. Many of the social reforms introduced were misunderstood, and people thought that their religion was in danger. The real need of the country was education. Had the sepoys of the Bengal Army been educated men, they would never have been misled by the absurd rumours which caused the revolt. Lack of education was the cause of the country's poverty. 'Look at England', he said. 'Look how her wealth has increased in the last century. She has had great difficulties to contend with—far greater than those which obstruct the spread of education in this country. In those days she had no railways, no steam printing-press—nothing but her own innate genius and unconquerable will.'

With the terrible tragedy of the Mutiny ever before his eyes, Saiyid Ahmed Khan set himself to what was to be his life work—the enlightenment of his fellow-countrymen. He thought that previous efforts made by such reformers as Lord Bentinck and Macaulay had failed because they were mainly directed towards the spread of English. English could never be the language of any but the few, and the masses could only be reached through their mother-tongue. Aided, therefore, by his friend and future biographer, Colonel Graham, he held a meeting of English and other Europeans at Ghazipur, the object of which was to found a society for translating useful works from English into Urdu. He also founded the Victoria College at Ghazipur for the same purpose. It was built entirely out of the contributions of the local inhabitants. In these endeavours he met with bitter opposition from local Muhammadans, who thought that Western ideas would undermine the religious beliefs of the young; but he stuck to his work with characteristic pluck. His efforts received much encouragement from the Viceroy, Lord Lawrence.

In 1869, Saiyid Ahmed Khan made a most courageous decision. His two sons had just been awarded State Scholarships, and were about to proceed to England. Although he was now fifty-two and knew little about English manners and social customs, he determined to accompany them. In January 1869, therefore, the party set out on the P. & O. steamer *Baroda*. His biographer tells us many amusing anecdotes about the voyage. Thus, one of his fellow passengers was describing the prosperity of the British Empire, which, he declared, was due to the Christian religion. Saiyid Ahmed Khan observed quietly that Jesus Christ was not a rich man.

In England he made many friends, including Thomas Carlyle. The Sage of Chelsea had long been interested in The Prophet, whom he had treated rather unfairly in his lectures on 'Heroes and Hero Worship'. Saiyid Ahmed was at the time engaged in bringing out his *Essays on the Life of Muhammed*, and the two talked together on the subject far into the night.

What impressed him most of all in England was the state of education of the people. His landlady would discuss politics with him, and the cabmen, waiting for their fares, read the daily newspaper. Even his maid-servant could read and write.

How different was all this from the state of things in India! 'The progress of the West,' he wrote to a friend, 'is entirely due to the fact that all the arts and sciences are treated of in languages they know. If they were taught in Latin, Greek, Persian or Arabic, the English would be in the same state of ignorance as that in which, I am sorry to say, the Hindu masses lie buried. Those who are bent on improving and bettering India must remember that the only way of compassing this is by having the whole of the arts and sciences translated into their own language. I should like to have this written in gigantic letters on the Himalayas for the remembrance of future generations.'

Soon after his return to India in 1870, Saiyid Ahmed Khan began to think out the details of a scheme for founding a residential college on the lines of Oxford and Cambridge, where the learning of East and West might be combined without prejudice to religion.

The Muhammadan Anglo-Oriental College Fund Committee was started in 1872, and four years later, Saiyid Ahmed Khan retired from Government service in order to devote his entire energies to the task. The foundation stone of the Muhammadan Anglo-Oriental College at Aligarh was laid in the following January by the Viceroy, Lord Lytton. The Aligarh College soon attracted students from all over India. Saiyid Ahmed Khan was fortunate to secure the services of such

Englishmen as Theodore Beck, Morison, and Sir Thomas Arnold; they freely mixed with their pupils and infected them with their own love of learning. Among the Indian scholars who made Aligarh their home were Hali, the Urdu poet; Shibli and Nazir Ahmad, the prose-writers; and Nawab Muhsinul Mulk, the great orator, who carried on Saiyid Ahmed's work after he died.

Saiyid Ahmed's aims went far beyond the Aligarh College. He started an annual Muhammadan Educational Conference, and many hundreds of Muslims attended in order to hear lectures on educational subjects. It led to the foundation of numbers of schools in different parts of the country. He was a master of Urdu prose, and edited a monthly periodical, *Tehzib-ul-Aklaq*, which dealt with questions of Social Reform in an uncompromising manner. 'I must say what is in my heart,' he declared, 'even at the risk of being distasteful.' But the work which brought a storm of opposition was his *Tafsir*, or Commentary on the Quran. Saiyid Ahmed wished to show that there was no opposition between the teaching of Islam and modern science, and his views on the subject were frankly rationalistic. He maintained that the Quran was not verbally inspired, but must be interpreted in the light of reason. The Ulema or Muhammadan theologians branded him as a Kafir or Infidel, and went to the length of obtaining a *fatwa* or religious edict against him from Mecca; his life was more than once in danger from the daggers of fanatics. But he went on calmly with his work, undeterred by praise or blame.

Saiyid Ahmed Khan served on the Legislative Council in the time of Lord Lytton, and again under Lord Ripon. He was a member of the Educational and the Public Services Commissions. When the Indian National Congress was formed, with his usual frankness, he would have nothing to do with it. This was not because he was a separatist, for no one was keener than he to see India a nation. The terms Hindu and Muhammadan were, he said, religious and not political terms. He even compared the two communities to the two eyes in a human body, both equally indispensable. Hindu students were admitted freely to Aligarh. But he thought that politics in a largely illiterate country would divert attention from the real need, which was education. For the same reason, he opposed Lord Ripon's scheme for Local Self-Government.

In 1887, Saiyid Ahmed Khan was made a K.C.S.I., and he devoted the remainder of his life to the causes he loved. The storms which attended the earlier part of his career had now blown over, and wherever he went his commanding figure, his long, snow-white beard, and his eloquent voice drew admiring crowds. No one was more loved and revered in Northern India. He died, full of years and honour, in 1898, and was laid to rest in a corner of the mosque of his beloved college. A fund raised to his memory in all parts of the country converted Aligarh into a University. It could not have been spent more fittingly. Perhaps his best epitaph is found in some lines written in his honour by the poet Hali:

To be ill treated by one's brethren, but to live
    for their good;
To love the arrow by which one is pierced;
To live with but one hope—to serve one's nation.
And to die with that hope in one's heart:
If *you* fulfil this ideal,
You can aspire to be a Saiyid Ahmed.

MAHATMA GANDHI

MOHANDAS KARAMCHAND GANDHI, perhaps the best known and most beloved Indian of to-day, was born at Porbandar in Kathiawar in October 1869. He was the youngest child of a large family. His father, who held a hereditary office in the State, was a man of very little education, and belonged to the Banya caste. Thus the Mahatma is truly a child of the people, and his sympathies have always been with victims of caste-tyranny and social injustice. According to the custom of the day, he was married at the age of thirteen, and this afterwards opened his eyes to the evils of child-marriage.

His earliest ambition was to be a lawyer, and for this purpose he went to England at the age of seventeen, in order to study at the Inner Temple. His experiences in England were not happy. In those days there were few Indians in the country, and he was a shy and lonely lad. He was impressed, however, by the superior physique of the English race, which he attributed to the fact that they ate meat. He thought that this was the reason why they were able to rule over a great country like India. Accordingly, young Gandhi determined to break the principles of the Jain religion in which he had been brought up, and become a meat-eater too. Soon, however, he abandoned the experiment in disgust, and returned to the simple vegetarian diet of his people. In due course, he was called to the Bar and returned to India. On his arrival, he had to submit to various rites in order to be readmitted to his caste. He learned on landing that his beloved mother had died during his absence; this filled him with grief, and for a long time he was inconsolable.

Gandhi, however, did not make a good pleader. When he took his first case in the Bombay Court he broke down completely, and was unable to proceed. He returned to Kathiawar, where for a time he helped his brother. It appeared as though he was to be a complete failure. But just as his fortunes were at their lowest the turning-point came. A large number of Indians had settled in South Africa. Many of these were the descendants of Indian coolies who had arrived in Natal under indenture to work when the colony was short of native labour. Others were Gujarathi merchants and traders, both Hindu and Moslem. Colour prejudice in South Africa was very strong, particularly in the Boer republics. The Boers, Dutch settlers, in spite of the protests of the British Government, had done all they could to restrict the free entry of Indians, and to prevent them from taking out licences to trade. In 1893, Gandhi went to South Africa on behalf of an Indian firm which had a legal dispute with the South African Republic, and his eyes were opened for the first time to the injustices which his countrymen were enduring. After the legal case was settled, Gandhi took up the question of the treatment of Indians by the Boers, and in 1896 he returned to India to lay the facts before the Indian Government. Meanwhile, an agitation was started by the English colonists of Natal against the importation of any more Indian labourers, as it was feared that they would lower the standard of living and the high rate of wages which the white men enjoyed. When Gandhi returned to South Africa in 1896, serious riots broke out. He was assaulted by an unruly mob, and was only rescued with difficulty.

Gandhi, however, remained loyal to the British Government. In 1899, war broke out between them and the Boers, as both parties claimed control over South Africa, and the Boers resented the presence of the Uitlanders or foreigners, who came in large numbers to the city of Johannesburg in order to exploit the gold mines. The Boers invaded Natal, and laid siege to the town of Ladysmith. General Buller was sent with an army to relieve it. Gandhi raised and trained a body of Indian stretcher-bearers, which was attached to General Buller's force. The Boers were excellent marksmen, who hid in the 'kopjes' or rocky heights and shot down the British soldiers without suffering any harm themselves. At a place called Colenso, a part of the British artillery had to be abandoned owing to heavy fire from these invisible.

foes, and the only son of Lord Roberts, Commander-in-Chief of the British Forces in South Africa, was killed. The Indian stretcher-bearers helped to remove the wounded soldiers and take them back to hospital. Some time later, the British seized a height called Spion Kop which overlooked Ladysmith, and they hoped by this means to open the way into the town, which was almost at its last gasp. But the Boers counter-attacked fiercely, and the British were forced to abandon the position. The fire was very heavy, and a hail of bullets came over the hill and fell on the farther side. But in spite of this, Gandhi and his stretcher-bearers worked calmly on, carrying the wounded to the base, where they could be properly cared for.

In the end, Ladysmith was relieved, and Lord Roberts and Lord Kitchener forced the brave Boers to surrender. The South African Union was formed, and British and Dutch gradually settled down in peace with equal civil rights. In 1901, the situation seemed so much better that Gandhi once more returned to his beloved motherland. He hoped that once the Boers were conquered the anti-Indian legislation would be repealed, and that Indians would no longer be made to pay the emigration tax and register their fingerprints, or submit to other restrictions. But this did not happen, and Gandhi again went to South Africa to champion the Indian cause. On his return, he founded the Transvaal British Indian Association, and started a newspaper called *Indian Opinion*.

About this time, he began to read a number of books which were destined to have a profound effect upon his outlook on life. Among these were Ruskin's *Unto This Last* and the works of the Russian reformer Tolstoy. From these studies he became convinced that true happiness can only be enjoyed by a return to a simple mode of life, and by giving up worldly ambitions. His religious outlook was formed largely on his studies of the Hindu *Bhagavad Gita* and Jesus's Sermon on the Mount. These, combined with the Jain creed on which he was brought up, taught him that a man's duty is to love his enemies, to do good to those who persecute him, and to refrain from taking life. The latter doctrine, known in Indian philosophy as *Ahimsa*, became a cardinal principle in Gandhi's life.

Gandhi now established a little colony of Indian and European friends who lived the simple life which he had laid down, and when the Government of South Africa still refused to give Indians the rights to which they felt they were entitled, he started a campaign of passive resistance.

Gandhi and other Indian leaders were arrested and thrown into prison; but the agitation created among the Indian community was so strong that the Government was compelled to agree to a compromise. Some of the Indians thought that Gandhi had betrayed their cause, and he was attacked and nearly murdered by a Pathan. Still, however, the South African Government seemed unwilling to grant all that it had promised, especially the repeal of an annual tax of £3 to be paid by all ex-indentured Indian settlers. In 1913 Gandhi therefore led a great march of Natal Indian indentured labourers, who were ready to go to prison rather than submit. The struggle only ended in 1914, when the 'Black Act', which obliged all Asiatic settlers to register their names with fingerprints, was repealed, together with the annual tax; and Indian marriages were legalized. Thus the legal status of Indians in South Africa was at last fully safeguarded.

In 1914, his work for his fellow-countrymen in South Africa having been successfully completed, Gandhi left with the good wishes of both Europeans and Indians, whose hearts he had won over to accept an agreement honourable to both parties. In India, he was accorded a triumphant reception during a prolonged tour which he undertook shortly after his return. He then turned his attention to the foundation of an Ashram or hermitage near Ahmedabad, where he and his followers could practise the kind of life he had planned for himself, unhampered by caste or creed. The admission of members of the depressed classes to his community led to a violent outcry from orthodox Hindu circles, which was only stopped when Gandhi threatened to leave the Ashram and go to dwell in the untouchable quarter himself. During this period, Gandhi still kept up the fight to stop the practice of sending indentured Indian labourers to work in foreign countries. He also intervened successfully in Bihar, where the European indigo-planters were treating their cultivators very badly; and when a famine broke out in the Kaira district, he urged the cultivators not to pay their land revenue until their grievances had been duly redressed. Many of the farmers allowed their goods and cattle to be seized, and even threatened to remove their standing crops.

But Gandhi's most successful feat was his intervention on behalf of the mill hands in Ahmedabad. They were overworked and underpaid, and in many cases they lived under deplorable conditions, crowded together in insanitary tenements. Gandhi exhorted them to strike for better treatment, and when this failed, he undertook to fast, to death if need be, until their grievances were remedied. This was the first time that Gandhi used in a dispute his famous weapon of *Satyagraha* or Soul Force. It was singularly successful: the mill owners gave way, and the conditions of the mill hands was materially improved in many respects. About this time, the title of *Mahatma*, or Great Soul, began to be applied to Gandhi as the champion of the poor and oppressed.

In 1914, the war with Germany broke out, and just as fifteen years earlier Gandhi had supported the British against the Boers, so on this occasion he volunteered his services for what he held to be the right cause. He worked hard to recruit a labour corps in Gujarat, and was awarded the

Kaisar-i-Hind medal for his services. After the war, India was in a very disturbed condition. The failure of the monsoon, the economic depression which made it impossible for the peasants to sell their crops, and the flooding of the labour market with thousands of disbanded soldiers had created much discontent.

An act known as the Rowlatt Act had been passed, enabling the Government to deal summarily with the Bengal anarchists, and there was widespread fear that its powers might be abused for the purpose of suppressing genuine political agitation. The Muhammadan community also was greatly perturbed by the harsh treatment of Turkey after the war, and the Afghans were threatening to invade India. Serious riots had broken out in various parts of the country, especially in the Punjab. At Amritsar, the mob had got completely out of hand. Two bank officials were burnt to death; the railway station was destroyed and the staff murdered. Martial law was proclaimed, and General Dyer, who was in charge, opened fire on a meeting which was being held in an enclosed space known as the Jalianwallah Bagh, killing and wounding a very large number of people.

General Dyer's conduct was made the subject of an enquiry, and he was placed on the retired list by way of punishment for having exceeded his powers. But the Jalianwallah Bagh shooting sent a wave of indignation through the entire country, and Gandhi, by way of protest, organized a movement known as non-cooperation with Government. People were to give up all titles and honorary offices; no Indian was to accept paid appointments or to serve Government in any capacity; everyone was to decline to pay taxes and to refuse to make use of the Government law-courts, schools, colleges and hospitals; and the police, army and excise officers and men were to refuse to work. Gandhi set an example by returning to the Viceroy his Kaisar-i-Hind medal.

Gandhi now became closely associated with the Indian National Congress. This political organization was founded in 1885, because at that time there were no bodies in the country to represent Indian political opinion; and it was drawn from representatives of all classes. It held meetings once a year, when resolutions were drawn up, calling the attention of Government to various grievances. It took a prominent part in the agitation against Lord Curzon's partition of Bengal in 1905, and ever since then it has been strongly nationalist in its outlook, and has aimed at securing the ultimate independence of the country from foreign rule. Gandhi quickly became a recognized leader of the Congress, though there were some others, like Pandit Motilal Nehru and Mr. R. C. Das, who did not agree with his politics, while they had the highest respect for his saintly character.

Gandhi, supported by the Congress Party, at

first decided to start a civil disobedience movement as a protest against the behaviour of General Dyer, but events proved that the masses were as yet unready for non-violence. In 1921, when the Prince of Wales landed in Bombay on a visit to India, there were riots in which almost as many lost their lives as at Jalianwallah Bagh. In the following year, at Chauri Chaura in the Gorakhpur District, a body of non-cooperators attacked twenty policemen and burnt them to death. There was also much bloodshed in the Punjab, and Gandhi himself was arrested and put on trial. He took full responsibility for what had happened and the judge with great reluctance sentenced him to six years' imprisonment. He was sent to Yeravda Jail, near Poona, where he was courteously treated. Two years later, he developed acute appendicitis. He was successfully operated on by the English Civil Surgeon of Poona and the unexpired portion of his sentence was commuted.

After his release from jail, Gandhi worked steadily to prepare the nation for non-violent civil disobedience. This meant the cultivation of the utmost self-restraint in the face of provocation, however severe; the non-cooperator was to learn to stand up cheerfully and calmly to *lathi* charges, beating, shooting and imprisonment without resistance. At the same time Gandhi had a definite programme for the social and economic regeneration of India. The use of foreign cloth was to be discontinued in favour of *khaddar* or homespun; everyone was to spin a stated number of yards of cotton every day, and to take a vow to use nothing but *swadeshi* or home-made articles. The manufacture of intoxicating liquor was to be stopped. Above all, the great curse of untouchability, which separated the members of the depressed classes from their fellow-Hindus and prevented them from living inside the villages or using the same temples and wells, was to be removed. In 1924, Gandhi became President of the Congress, and his followers adopted as their badge the little white cap of *khaddar*, modelled on the convict's cap which their leader had been forced to wear in jail in South Africa.

In 1926, Lord Irwin became Viceroy of India. He was a great and good man, with deep religious convictions, and between him and the Mahatma there quickly arose a deep mutual respect and regard. But Gandhi was still determined to right the various wrongs and disabilities under which his people were suffering. One of these was the tax on salt, which, he thought, weighed very heavily on the poorest classes. As a symbolic protest against this, he started a march to the seashore at Dandi in Gujarat in order to defy the Government by making salt out of sea-water. The march to Dandi soon became a triumphant procession. As soon as Gandhi left his *Ashram* on the banks of the Sabarmati, he was joined by hundreds of followers. At almost every village, the *patels* or village officers laid down their offices, even though they knew that their lands would be forfeited. The movement reached such dimensions that Government found it necessary to order Gandhi's arrest, and he was once more lodged in Yeravda Jail.

Meanwhile, the English and Indian Governments were working hard to evolve a new constitution, which would prepare India for the day when she would receive Dominion Status, and be on the same footing as Canada, Australia, New Zealand or South Africa, as a self-governing nation within the Empire. But it was difficult to arrive at a solution which would at the same time satisfy the Indian Princes, the Congress leaders, the Muslims, and the various minority communities. The matter had already been investigated by a Parliamentary Commission under Sir John Simon, a distinguished lawyer and statesman; but the Commission consisted entirely of Englishmen, and its findings were not accepted by Indian politicians. In November 1930, a Round Table Conference, consisting of Indian and English members, was called in London to discuss the whole question; but Congress was not represented, as the Civil Disobedience movement was then at its height, and most of the leaders were in jail.

Lord Irwin was determined to remedy this state of affairs. He was anxious that Gandhi should attend the next session of the Conference as the Congress representative, and in January 1931 he released the members of the Working Committee who were in prison. In February, Gandhi went to Delhi to see Lord Irwin, and after prolonged discussions an agreement was signed; Government was to withdraw its depressive measures, and Congress was to call off Civil Disobedience. Gandhi was to attend the second session of the Conference, and accordingly he sailed for London in the following October. It is characteristic of the man that while in London he lodged in a working class district among the very poor, and in spite of the cold he continued to wear only the simple loin cloth of *khaddar* in which he was clad in India.

I do not think that Gandhi was quite at home in the atmosphere of the Round Table Conference. He was ill at ease among statesmen and politicians, as his heart was really with the millions of poverty-stricken Indian peasants in his native land. For this reason he did not contribute very much to the discussions. The Conference did not seem to him to be representative of India. 'I, who am representing over ninety per cent of the Indian population,' he said, ' am pitted against one hundred and forty-nine or whatever is the number of other delegates. Immediately I make good that claim, you will see that my task before the Conference and the British Ministers will be easier. Unless I prove that the Congress represents the bulk of the people, I must go back and restart Civil Disobedience.'

But Gandhi did valuable work outside the

Conference, in making the various classes of people in England acquainted with Indian aspirations and demands. He visited the Universities, the famous Public School at Eton, the Lancashire millworkers, the Committee Room of the House of Commons and other places, and everywhere he was listened to with the closest attention.

The second session of the Round Table Conference went on till December, but nothing very definite emerged, as the delegates were unable to reach a decision on the all-important question of communal representation on the Legislative Councils. Gandhi refused to consider a separate electorate for any community except the Muslims, the Sikhs and the Europeans; as regards the depressed classes, he insisted that they were Hindus, and must be kept within the Hindu fold. Dr. Ambedkar, the leader of the depressed classes, took the opposite point of view. When the Conference was wound up on 1 December, the Prime Minister, Mr. Ramsay MacDonald, announced that as no agreement had been reached he himself would be obliged to make a Communal award.

On 5 December, Gandhi left Victoria Station amid enthusiastic scenes. He stopped at Paris, where he met Romain Rolland, the famous author and pacifist, who afterwards wrote his biography. He also went to Lausanne in Switzerland, and to Rome where he had an interview with Signor Mussolini. His message to the people was always the same 'Europe,' he repeatedly declared, ' is suffering from a malady caused by the burden of armaments, and most countries are on the verge of moral and material bankruptcy.' Events have shown that his words were prophetic.

Gandhi sailed from Brindisi by the Italian steamer *Pilsna* on 13 December, and arrived in Bombay on the 28th. He was accorded an enthusiastic reception and enormous crowds assembled on the Maidan to hear him speak. But he found the country in a desperate condition. There were complaints on the part of the Government that Congress leaders had broken the truce in his absence; Congress on the other hand declared that Government had started 'legalized terrorism' by imposing ordinances on Bengal and the North-West Frontier, and by taxing the *ryots* in the United Provinces. Gandhi asked for an interview with the Viceroy, which was refused; whereupon Congress threatened to renew Civil Disobedience unless Government repealed the ordinances and left them free scope to prosecute their claim for complete independence. Government thereupon arrested Gandhi and other leaders, and took stern steps to repress the threatened outbreak. Many thousands of the followers of Congress were thrown into prison.

In August, the Prime Minister's communal decision was received, and it was announced that the various communities would have separate representation in the Legislative Councils. Gandhi thought that this would divide the whole country, and he announced that he would 'fast unto death' unless the method of representation provided for the depressed classes was altered. Mr Gandhi's fast at Yeravda Jail began on 20 September and caused widespread concern. It was felt that the Mahatma was no longer a young man and the consequences might well be fatal. Anxious crowds waited day and night outside the door of the prison. Great was the relief when it was announced that a compromise, known as the Poona Pact, was arrived at, and the Mahatma broke his fast on the 26th in the presence of a band of devoted followers.

In the following year, Gandhi undertook two more fasts in order to melt the hearts of the high-caste Hindus, who were still opposed to giving the untouchable classes their rights. The first was a three weeks' fast beginning on 8 May, and as soon as it started Government released their distinguished prisoner, who was taken to the neighbouring mansion of a wealthy Hindu admirer and treated with loving care. The fast ended on 29 May, and the patient slowly recovered.

After he had regained his strength, Gandhi decided to abandon mass disobedience, for which he felt that the country was still unfitted. He substituted an individual movement, and in order to start it he revived his old plan of a march through the country, accompanied by his followers. He was once more arrested and imprisoned. In August, finding that the authorities did not afford him proper facilities for prosecuting his work on behalf of the Untouchables, he again went on hunger-strike, and this time he was released unconditionally.

Meanwhile, the work on the Government of India Bill was going on. The Round Table Conferences came to an end, and a Joint Select Committee of Parliament was appointed to examine witnesses and ascertain what opinions Indians of various schools of thought held on its proposals. The Government of India Bill was a great advance on the past. The Provinces were to have complete autonomy, and at the Centre there was to be a Federal Government including representatives of the Provinces and the Indian States. But certain important powers, including control over the Army and Finance, were reserved to the Viceroy, and this by no means satisfied Congress politicians, who claimed full Dominion Status at once. Gandhi was never greatly interested in purely political questions, and he was busy at the time on an untouchability campaign. During his tour, large sums in cash and jewels were collected and devoted to securing better housing, schools and other benefits for these poor folk. In January 1934 occurred the terrible Bihar earthquake, and he gladly co-operated with the Government in collecting funds and organizing relief among the peasants, whose sufferings were terrible.

In 1935, the Government of India Bill was passed by both Houses of Parliament and became law. Owing, however, to difficulties with regard to the position of the Indian States, it was determined to apply the new constitution to the Provinces only. When the first elections were held, in eight out of the eleven provinces Congress representatives swept the board. Gandhi was opposed to the acceptance of office by Congress members, and for a time the Governors had to appoint ministers chosen by themselves. At length, however, the objection was overruled, and from 1937 to the outbreak of the present war, Congress ministers were in power. During that time, they accomplished a great amount of useful work. The sale of intoxicating drink was prohibited, and great strides were made in compulsory education, village uplift, and the various social services. About this time, Gandhi himself retired from active participation in politics, which he decided to leave to younger men, and he lives at the little village of Sevagram, near the town of Wardha in the Central Provinces, where his advice is eagerly sought on all sorts of political, social and religious questions. He enjoys the confidence and respect of the present Viceroy, Lord Wavell, just as he had formerly done that of Lord Irwin and Lord Linlithgow.

Such then in brief has been the career of the Gujarathi saint, who, in the words of his biographer, " has stirred three hundred million people to revolt, has shaken the foundations of the British Empire, and has introduced into human politics the strongest religious impulse of the last two thousand years ". His appearance is typical of the man. Frail and thin, with large eyes and a peculiarly winning smile and a loincloth of coarse *khaddar*, he would pass unnoticed in an Indian crowd save for a peculiarly arresting personality which at once attracts the beholder. Indeed, his body seems hardly to count at all. He sleeps little, works without ceasing, and lives on a diet of goats' milk and fruit. He has none of the arts of the orator, yet his simple words have a ring of passionate sincerity. Gentle and courteous in his dealings with his opponents, and always ready to admit a mistake, he is nevertheless as tough as steel where vital principles are at stake. He has introduced into political struggles a new factor which raises resistance to evil to a plane hitherto unknown; and it is even possible that one day in the not distant future, a distracted world will find that the true solution of its difficulties lies in the principles enunciated by Mahatma Gandhi.